To:

Thank you for your friendship!

From:

Everyone needs a friend to lean on:
David Neate

Numbers 6:24-26
The LORD bless you and keep you; the LORD make his
face shine upon you and be gracious to you; the LORD
turn his face towards you and give you peace. (NIV)

County Antrim: Liz Edwards

Philemon 1:4

I always thank my God as I remember
you in my prayers… (NIV)

Friendship is the inexpressible comfort of
feeling safe with a person,
having neither to weigh thoughts
nor measure words.

George Eliot
English novelist, 1819 -1880

•

Friendship is unnecessary,
like philosophy, like art...
It has no survival value; rather it is one of those
things that give value to survival.

C.S. Lewis
Irish writer, 1898 -1963

•

There is no surer foundation for a beautiful
friendship than a mutual taste in literature.

P.G. Wodehouse
English writer, 1881-1975

I would rather walk with a friend in
the dark, than alone in the light.
Helen Keller
American deaf-blind writer and advocate
for the disabled, 1880-1968

Portsmouth Sunset: Jonathan Leach

Friendly Swans: Kevin Meilak

Friendship is one of the sweetest joys of life.
Many might have failed beneath the bitterness
of their trial had they not found a friend.
Charles Haddon Spurgeon
British clergyman, 1834 -1892

It is more fun to talk with someone who doesn't use long, difficult words but rather short, easy words like "What about lunch?"

From Winnie-the-Pooh
by A.A. Milne, 1882-1956

•

Forget about housework, a real friend comes to visit you not your house!

Cushendun, Northern Ireland: Liz Edwards

A true friend makes themselves at home in your kitchen and puts the kettle on without asking!

●

The ornament of a house is the friends who frequent it.

Ralph Waldo Emerson
American poet, 1803 - 1882

Snow over Jevington,
East Sussex: John Flude

Don't walk in front of me, I may not follow;
Don't walk behind me, I may not lead;
Walk beside me, and just be my friend.
Albert Camus
French philosopher, 1913-1960

A Single Flower: Geraint Wyn Jones

The greatest good you can do
for another
is not just share your riches,
but to reveal to him, his own.

Benjamin Disraeli
British Prime Minister to Queen Victoria,
1804-1881

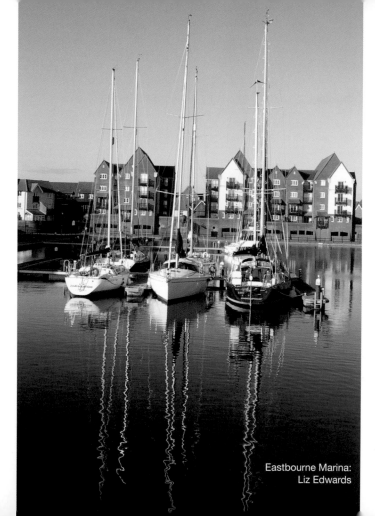

Eastbourne Marina:
Liz Edwards

Proverbs 27:19
A mirror reflects a man's face,
but what he is really like is shown by the kind
of friends he chooses.
(The Living Bible)

•

3 John 1:2
My dear friend, I pray that everything
may go well with you and that you may be
in good health – as I know you are well in spirit.
(Good News Bible)

My best friend is the one who brings out
the best in me.
Henry Ford
American businessman, 1863 - 1947

●

Calories don't count when you are enjoying
supper with a friend.

●

The best vitamin for making friends – B1

●

Good friends are like an excellent wine,
they get better with age.

Campanula: Liz Edwards

When we honestly ask ourselves which person in
our lives means the most to us,
we often find that it is those who, instead of
giving advice, solutions, or cures,
have chosen rather to share our pain and touch
our wounds with a warm and tender hand.

Henri Nouwen
Dutch Clergyman, 1932 - 1996

Tulip Fields: Alan Lambert

Wishing to be friends is quick work,
but friendship is a slow ripening fruit.
Aristotle
Greek philosopher 384-322 BC

●

Nothing but heaven itself is better than
a friend who is really a friend.
Plautus
Roman writer, 254-184 BC

●

Friendship improves happiness
and abates misery,
by the doubling of our joy and the
dividing of our grief.
Cicero
Roman statesman, 106 – 43 BC

Winter Sunset: Claire Hookey

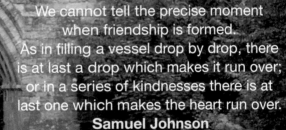

We cannot tell the precise moment
when friendship is formed.
As in filling a vessel drop by drop, there
is at last a drop which makes it run over;
or in a series of kindnesses there is at
last one which makes the heart run over.
Samuel Johnson
English author, 1709 - 1784

Kirkby Lonsdale, Cumbria: Paul Matthews

Cheeky Robin: Mike Williams

Friends are those rare people who
ask how you are and then wait
to hear the answer.

●

The miracle of friendship can be
spoken without words... hearing
unspoken needs, recognizing secret
dreams, understanding the silent
things that only true friends know.

Anon

Let us be grateful to people
who make us happy;
they are the charming gardeners
who make our souls blossom.

Marcel Proust
French author, 1871 - 1922

●

A true friend is someone who thinks that
you are a good egg
even though he knows that you are
slightly cracked!

Bernard Meltzer
American radio host, 1916 - 1998

Late Summer Flowers: Liz Edwards

It's the friends you can call
up at 4am that matter.
Marlene Dietrich
American actress, 1901-1992

Country Landscape: Mike Williams

The gift of friendship...
A willingness to listen...
A pair of helping hands...
A whisper from the heart...
The knowledge that someone
cares and understands.

It is one of the blessings of old
friends that you can afford to be stupid
with them.

Ralph Waldo Emerson
American poet, 1803 -1882

•

A best friend is somebody who knows
every last thing about you,
yet still manages to like you anyway.

Sunset over Southampton Water: Chris Fay

If a man does not make new
acquaintances as he advances
through life,
he will soon find himself left alone.
A man, Sir, should keep his
friendship in constant repair.
Samuel Johnson
English author, 1709 -1784

Autumn Woods: Anne Blair-Vincent

The friend who can be silent with us in a
moment of despair or confusion,
who can stay with us in an hour of grief
and bereavement,
who can tolerate not knowing,
not caring, not healing –
and face with us the reality of
our powerlessness –
that is the friend who really cares.

Anon

●

As medicine is to the body,
so your friendship is to my soul

Friendship: Sue Percey

But every memory of friendship shared,
even for a short time, is a treasure,
like sunshine and warmth in our lives,
like a cool breeze on a humid day,
like a shower of rain refreshing the earth...
Anon

Giant's Causeway Meadow: Liz Edwards

Christmas Snow: Mike Williams

Proverbs 17:17
Friends love through all kinds of weather
and families stick together
in all kinds of trouble.
(The Message)

•

Lots of people want to ride with you in the
limo, but a true friend will take the bus with
you when the limo breaks down.
Oprah Winfrey
American TV presenter, 1954 - present

A friend is one that knows you as you are,
understands where you have been,
accepts what you have become,
and still, gently allows you to grow.

William Shakespeare
English playwright, 1564-1616

●

Treat your friends as you do your pictures, and
place them in their best light!

Jennie Churchill
1854 –1921, Mother of Winston Churchill.

Poppy Field:
Jonathan Leach

A Pooh-sticks bridge: Paul Matthews

'We'll be Friends Forever, won't we, Pooh?' asked Piglet.
'Even longer,' Pooh answered.
A.A. Milne
children's author, 1882-1956

May God's blessing surround you
each day,
As you trust him and walk in his way,
May his presence within,
Guard and keep you from sin,
Go in peace, go in joy, go in love.

Cliff Barrows
Music Director for the
Billy Graham
Evangelistic Association

●

Please remember that you
are MY friend and I am so
thankful for all the times
we have shared together.